HOLLYWOOD

SINISTER PEDOPHILIA

Are Steven Spielberg and friends,

Kevin Spacey, Dustin Hoffman,

Andrew Kreisberg, Bryan Singer, the

Weinstein brothers, Roman Polanski,

part of a Hollywood Pedophiles ring?

Table of Contents

Number 5: Pedophile Jones 7

Number 4: Crispin Glover thinks Spielberg is a pedophile..................15

Number 3: likes little boys 19

Number 2: child stars and protégées 45

Number 1: Hollywood whispers...54

Kevin Spacey Dustin Hoffman Andrew Kreisberg Bryan Singer the Weinstein brothers and many others are now facing public scrutiny after being accused of crimes ranging from: sexual harassment, sexual assault, to the rape of minors.

Former Hollywood child stars are finally starting to speak out about the pedophilic pandemic that plagues Hollywood. Plenty of disturbing rumors are spreading about certain film studios acting as money launderers for child pornography and sadistic ritual abuse and trafficking of children. It's interesting what we find when we examine those at the very top of the Hollywood Hill.

Here are five creepy facts that reveal a dark and sinister side of Steven Spielberg.

Number 5: Pedophile Jones

Your favorite action hero is a pedophile. There's a transcription of a pre-production story meeting for the first *Indiana Jones* film that is very fascinating. *The Raiders of the Lost Ark's* story meeting is between George Lucas Steven Spielberg and Lawrence Kasdan and if you read it you literally are witnessing the birth of Indiana Jones.

Not only do you get to see how they work out the story and characters, you also get to see things that were nuggets that were used in *Temple of Doom*.

And there's even some shades of The Last Crusade. But the biggest highlight from the transcription is how they planned for Indiana Jones to have a pedophilic relationship with Marion.

George Lucas: *"I was thinking that the old guy could have been his mentor. He could have known this little girl when she was just a kid. Had an affair with her when she was 11."*

Lawrence Kasdan: *"And he was 42."*

George Lucas: *"He hasn't seen her in 12 years. Now she's 22. It's a real strange relationship."*

Steven Spielberg: "She had better be older than 22."

Georges Lucas: *"He's 35 and he knew her 10 years ago when he was 25 and she was only 12. It would be amusing to make her slightly young at the time."*

Steven Spielberg: *"And promiscuous she came on to him."*

George Lucas: "15 is right on the edge. I know it's an outrageous idea, but it is interesting. Once she is 16 or 17 it's not interesting anymore. But if she was 15 and he was 25 and they actually had an affair the last time they me. And she was madly in love with him and he ..." Keeping this transcription in mind this scene becomes a lot more sinister:

Indiana: Hello, Marion.

Marion: Indiana Jones. I always knew some day you'd come walking back through my door. I never doubted that. Something made it inevitable. So, what are you doing here in Nepal?

Indiana: I need one of the pieces your father collected.

[*Marion surprises him with a right cross to the jaw*]

Marion: I've learned to hate you in the last ten years!

Indiana: I never meant to hurt you.

Marion: I was a child. I was in love. It was wrong and you knew it!

Indiana: You knew what you were doing.

Marion: Now I do. This is my place. Get out!

Indiana: I did what I did you don't have to be happy about it but maybe we can help each other out now.

Indiana Jones had sexual intercourse with an 11 or 12 year old girl.

It was justified by making it seem like the child was the promiscuous one who came onto Indiana Jones. And, I quote "knew exactly what she was doing" sounds like the defense Quentin Tarantino made to excuse Roman Polanski from raping a 13 year old girl. And this becomes extremely suspicious when you take into consideration the Polanski versus Samantha game case. On the 10th of March 1977 Polanski, then aged 43, became embroiled in a sexual assault case involving a 13 year old girl, Samantha Jane Gailey:

A grand jury charged Polanski with five charges:

One: rape by use of drugs

Two: perversion

Three: sodomy

Four: lewd and lascivious act upon a child under 14

Five: furnishing a controlled substance to a minor.

This ultimately led to Polanski's guilty plea to a different charge of lawful sexual intercourse with a minor.

This took place on the 10th of March 1977, at the home of actor Jack Nicholson in the Mulholland area of Los Angeles. At the time the crime was committed Nicholson was on a ski trip in Colorado. And just to make things a little weirder, here's a picture of Roman Polanski and Steven Spielberg on a little ski trip in 1977:

Steven Spielberg, Roman Polanski and Sissy Spacek. Avoriaz, 1977.

Translate from Romanian

9:02 AM - 26 Jan 2016

If Spielberg was skiing buddies with Polanski there is a good chance that he knew of his sexual perversions, and the inclusion of a pedophilic relationship in *Indiana Jones* was a nod to the disgraced director.

When the film was adapted to a novel Campbell Black created more of a backstory and used the actual age difference of the actors he determined that the Marion and Indiana affair happened when she was 15 and Indie was 24. But even in that case, Indie still slept with a minor.

Number 4: Crispin Glover thinks Spielberg is a pedophile

Crispin Glover played Marty McFly's father in Back to the Future and was supposed to return for the sequel, however, he turned down the part and later sued Spielberg and one: for using his likeness in the film. The reason why Crispin left is still unclear as the reason he gives have changed several times.

From the story being morally corrupt, to payment issues, no one can be really certain... However, Crispin Glover wrote an essay on his website which has unfortunately been deleted but can be found on archives on the Wayback machine and is referenced through several articles. This essay suggests that Steven Spielberg likes little boys and Hollywood is covering up for him.

What is it? by Crispin Hellion Glover

"*Does Steven Spielberg holds the same values I wish upon myself? Does the mind of this grinning bespectacled baseball capped man entirely reflect this culture? Is it true that in his waning years Orson Welles asked Steven Spielberg for a small amount of money with which he could make a final film? Is it true Steven Spielberg refused? Is it true Steven Spielberg bought a sled used in Citizen Kane for an extremely large sum of money? Do Steven Spielberg's passions burn?*

Do passions burn in the man now imprisoned who wished to anally rape Steven Spielberg? Do our cultural mouthpieces confidently inform us that the wish to anally raped Steven Spielberg is a bad thought? Could anal rape of Steven Spielberg be simply the manifestation of a cultural mandate? Do you believe Steven Spielberg is an ideal guide and influence for our culture? What do Steven Spielberg's films question? Does Steven Spielberg focused much of his fantasy life on young people? Did he portrayed children wallowing in sewers filled with fecal matter in Schindler's List? Did he use children to finger paint an adult in Hook? Does he collect the illustrations of Norman Rockwell such as the ones showing a young boy in his underwear examined by a doctor? Are the inclinations of Steven Spielberg above suspicion by the media fed culture?

Was Steven Spielberg very friendly with Michael Jackson? Wasn't Michael Jackson supposed to play Peter Pan in Steven Spielberg's version of the story? Do Michael Jackson and Steven Spielberg share similar opinions about the sexuality?"

Number 3: likes little boys

- *Cut*

- *Awful!*

- *who are you?*

- *The name's Iris Seagull. I directed the episode of Sybil where Christine Baranski sat on her balls… point is. I can direct this thing!*

- *Look how many pockets are on his jacket! I think we should let him do it.*

- *I'll remake mannequin on one condition: we make it Goonies.*

- *The Goonies why?*

- *Look at you four fat nerdy smart-mouthed Asian, you guys are the Goonies!*

- *What's good enough for you with good enough for me it's good enough for me!*

Crispin Glover isn't the only one who thinks that Steven Spielberg likes little boys.

The NAMBLA bulletin has a special column called "boys in the media" tracking the doings of such Hollywood chickens as Macaulay Culkin, known affectionately in the bulletin as Mac. The self-described ganymedian L. Martin who wrote "The boys in the media column" spoke by phone about Steven Spielberg and *Hook*. Chicken is a term originally coined by NAMBLA "the North American man-boy lovers Association" that describes an underage male sexual partner which was exposed by a decide man in his documentary that exposes the group called Chicken Hawk men who love little boys.

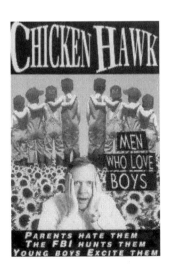

"Spielberg is known for his interest in young boys," *"certainly,"* said Martin, *"a lot of the members have been talking about Hook telling me how much they enjoyed it."* NAMBLA spokesman Renato Kurata refused to confirm or deny Spielberg's possible membership in the man-boy love Association: *"we do not divert all our membership rolls."* A lot of Spielberg's films focus on a man and boy relationship and Spielberg has been accused of trying to desensitize people to the notion of children having unusual close relationships with strange men or strange beings...

For instance,

E.T.

Back to the Future,

Jurassic Park,

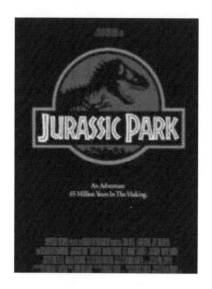

Indiana Jones and the Temple of Doom,

AI,

Temple of the Sun,

The adventures of Tintin,

The Goonies,

And even *Hook*,

Michael Jackson was set to play Peter Pan in Spielberg's adaptation of the classic children's story which was written by yet another alleged

boy lover James M Barrie.

But Jackson was dropped and recast without explanation and soon

after the pedophile allegations started coming in. During this time

it was rumored that Michael Jackson had refused to renew his

contract with Sony epic and was threatening them with a lawsuit.

Corey Feldman also claims he went to the FBI to name a few very powerful Hollywood pedophiles but the FBI refused to investigate and instead focus their attention on Michael Jackson.

Tristar, a Sony company, was also the studio behind the production of Steven Spielberg's *Hook*. Steven Spielberg's adaptation replaced the Forever Young Peter Pan with an older man, yet again, sticking to his man-boy relationship formula. Spielberg's costume designer, Anthony Powell, who also worked with Roman Polanski, endows *Hook*'s Lost Boys with Benetton meets Oliver Twist look tailor-made for the chicken's hawk sensibility *"Dance of the Warriors"*

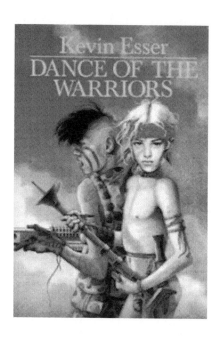

a futuristic fantasy about a warrior cult of young boys, who fight right-wing Christians for the privilege of having sex with aging boy lovers… sports on its cover a salt-and-pepper boy couple

who almost precisely mirrored two of Spielberg's Lost Boys. The book appeared in the pedophilia section of gay bookstores

Dance of the Warriors
by Kevin Esser

★★★☆ 3.72 · Rating details · 4 Ratings · 1 Review

It's the middle of the 21st Century. Medieval militarism has reduced America to a wasteland of failing crops and decaying cities. Gays and boylovers are packed off to detention camps in Utah. The only rebels are "vags," young male warriors living in such abandoned reaches as North Chicago. Ultimately, this is the uplifting odyssey of two boys, 13-yr-old Teddy and his frien ...more

just at the time that *Hook* was going into pre-production.

Hook's emotional highlight

strangely absent from the shooting scripts first revised draft, is the touchy-feely communion of the adult Peter Pan and the lost boys, were treated to prolonged takes of the tykes touching and caressing Robin Williams face and body.

When The Lost Boys smear war paint on Williams naked torso, the Idyll is reminiscent of a certain gay body painting video advertised in *The Advocate* that focuses on creative eroticism that expands and extends the beauty of foreplay.

Even if we are reading a bit too deep into this it's not hard to miss some of the rather odd tones and scenes from his movies. *"And he slashes at you with this*

6-inch retractable claw like a razor on the middle toe. He doesn't bother to bite you Jack you look like a lion you see, he slashes at you here, or here, or maybe across the belly spilling your intestines the point is... you are alive when they start to meet you. So you know better show a little respect".

Especially his first movie which is now the name of his own production studio Amblin.

In Amblin, a young man carrying a closely guarded guitar case befriends a free-spirited young woman while hitchhiking across the desert in southern California on route to the Pacific coast. At the beach, the man frolics in the surf while the woman covertly inspects the content of his guitar case, a suit and tie toothpaste, mouthwash, milk of magnesia, a roll of toilet paper, and a copy of Arthur c Clarke s' *This City and the Stars.*

The woman smiles in bemusement perhaps sensing all along that her companion was not the quintessential hippie that he appeared to be... She then leaves the beach without him. It doesn't sound that exciting right? But after Sid Sheinberg, the then vice-president of production for Universal Television, saw the film, Spielberg was signed to a seven-year contract with Universal television, making him the youngest director ever to get a long-term deal with a major studio.

What exactly is so special about this 26 minute film with no dialogue? It's a movie about pretending to be normal while keeping your secret close guarded. The reason why the girl left him on the beach is not because the guy wasn't a hippie, it was because he was gay and the evidence is in his guitar case.

Milk of Magnesia, and *The City and the Stars*, by Arthur c Clarke.

Let's take a look at the evidence starting with this city and the stars. Here's an analysis of the book from *Purple Prose Archive*:

The City and the Stars reflects the experience of someone who feels very different to everyone else around them. I can see how it would have appealed to disaffected adolescents in the 1950s. Alvin is not like anyone else on Earth, no one understands him, and he doesn't share their fears. He has to leave his supposed home to find his true home. I generally try and avoid making simplistic autobiographical links between stories and their writers, but as I read, I did find myself wondering if Arthur C. Clarke might have been gay. So when I looked him up on Wikipedia, I was interested to find out that he almost certainly was. Something about Alvin's subject position reminded me of being a gay adolescent myself – that feeling of being different to everyone else, wanting something they don't want, not to mention his inability to relate to his girlfriend and his close bond with Hilvar. I did find this undertone quite interesting and wondered if it might have contributed to the sense of emotional distancing in the novel.

On a trip to Florida in 1953 Clark met and quickly married Marilyn Mayfield, a 22 year old American divorcee with a young son. They separated permanently after six months although the divorce was not finalized until 1964. "The marriage was incompatible from the beginning," said Clark. Clark never remarried but was close to a Sri Lankan man, Leslie Akana Yaqui, whom Clark called his only perfect friend of a lifetime. In the dedication to his novel *The Fountains of Paradise*, Clark is buried with Akana Yaqui.

In his biography of Stanley Kubrick, John Baxter cites Clark's homosexuality as a reason why he relocated, due to more tolerant laws with regard to homosexuality in Sri Lanka. In an interview in the July 1986 issue of Playboy magazine, when asked if he had a bisexual experience, Clark stated "of course who hasn't". In his obituary Clark's friend Carrier Quinn wrote "yes Arthur was gay, as Isaac Asimov once told me." I think he simply found he preferred men. Arthur didn't publicize his sexuality, that wasn't the focus of his life, but if asked, he was open and honest. What's even more disturbing is that Arthur c. Clarke has strong ties to NAMBLA, and has been accused of being a pedophile by highly credible sources and despite condemning evidence, had never been charged.

U.S. detectives who arrested leaders of NAMBLA 10 years ago say Clark was named by other pedophiles they quizzed during the FBI investigation. The perverts had set up children homes in Thailand as a front for their sick activities.

One of its leaders was Jonathan Tampico, 48, a top nuclear scientist, who worked with the America government. He served two and a half years in jail for molesting a boy of 12 and is now on the run with a multi-million dollar warrant on his head for further porn offenses. He told detectives he had stayed at Clark's home in Colombo and had swapped letters with the author. Another known pedophile, former church minister John Wakefield Cummings, 56, is serving a 24 years to life sentence after admitting to molesting 17 boys in his care. He told the police in Sacramento California that Clark had been in contact at his Sri Lankan home by a pedophile who was on the run from American authorities.

In a sworn statement made to an investigator for Sacramento's District Attorney Wakefield Cummings told how the pervert fled to Sri Lanka where he was able to contact the pedophile community through Clark. Detectives contacted a child welfare group to warn them about Clark's activities.

A senior Sacramento detective said *"We never had any reason to take action against Arthur c Clarke because he was outside our jurisdiction but Clark's name did keep coming up we were looking into members of the boy lovers Association who all seem to know or beware of him he ended up connecting to a lot of people we were investigating. Tampico was one of those who said he went to Sri Lanka I have seen letters between him and Arthur c Clarke. There was nothing overtly sexual in them but they were clearly corresponding."* He added, "Cummings told us in the course of interviews that Arthur c Clarke is a pedophile.

He said 'Sri Lanka used to be a popular destination for pedophiles but then the government changed and they were all thrown out.' he said 'Clark was one of the few that didn't expel because of his status.' Ron O'Grady of ECPAT confirmed he had been warned about Clark by police in Sacramento.

So now that we can assume that the character in Amblin is gay, the milk of magnesia starts to make a whole lot of sense. *Milk of Magnesia* is a laxative that is often taken by gay men to clear their bowels before anal sex. Perhaps Spielberg was signaling to other Hollywood producers letting them know exactly what he's up for and what he's into. How did 20 year old Steven Spielberg get his $15,000 funding? An unknown man called Dennis Hoffman, produced his film, and he's never produced again. Also, the movie title *Amblin* is nonsensical, it has no meaning.

However, the name of the protagonist in Arthur c Clarke book is Alvin the major difference in the name is MB, could this stand for "man boy" in that case "man boy love". I mean Amblin and NAMBLA are very similar names or maybe it's just a shout out to the children of Hamblin:

The Chilling True Story Behind the Pied Piper of Hamelin

Could the legend of the Pied Piper hint at a real tragedy that befell the town of Hamelin more than 700 years ago?

you know, the ones who were stolen by the Pied Piper. It is also interesting to note that Steven Spielberg was on the advisory board of the Boy Scouts of America but decided to stop supporting them when they stood firm on the decision they would not accept gay people.

"I thought the Boy Scouts stood for equal opportunity and I have consistently spoken out publicly and privately against intolerance and discrimination based on ethnic religious racial and sexual orientation," Spielberg noted.

Joey Robinson, a spokesman for the Boy Scouts Los Angeles counsel, said he had not yet been informed that the filmmaker had departed his advisory role. He did however defend the council's right to set its membership policies: *"it's not discrimination it's the right to set membership standards,"* Robinson said. "Every group has its standards. The Girl Scouts have a rule that you have to be a girl." When asked how he felt about Spielberg's opposition to the group's policy excluding gays, Robinson said, *"this is America everybody has a right to voice their opinion and we respect his right."* The Boy Scouts begin accepting members at the young age of seven and on occasion, the Cub Scouts are included.

In senior Scout events in late 2017 the policy was revised and gay and transgender people are now allowed to join the Boy Scouts.

Number 2: child stars and protégées

Steven Spielberg is known as the creator of stars. Not only does he cast people for his roles but he also head hunts. He personally discovered drew Barrymore, Christian Bale, Alden Ehrenreich, and many others. He has also worked with a plethora of child actors who have now risen to international stardom. However a lot of the talents he has produced have all had issues growing up if they ever grew up at all.

Drew Barrymore first met her on-screen debut on Steven Spielberg's E.T. She developed a drinking and drug addiction at the age of nine, and was sent to rehab at the age of thirteen.

Corey Feldman who appeared in gremlins at the age of seven and later in the *Goonies*

claimed that he and his friend Corey Haim were drugged and raped by one of the most powerful men in Hollywood.

Corey Haim

although never featured in a Spielberg movie, was spotted on the set with Spielberg.

Feldman claims that Haim was raped by an A-list actor producer and director. Corey Haim died in 2010 after a drug overdose.

Elijah Wood *

was only eight when he appeared in Steven Spielberg's *Back to the Future 2*. He also claims that he was molested and raped as a child and that the most powerful men in Hollywood are pedophiles.

Judith Barsi appeared in Spielberg's *Jaws 2* and *The Land that Time Forgot,* who died at the age of 10, in an alleged murder-suicide, she was shot and set on fire.

She was buried with her mother in an unmarked grave and her father's body disappeared.

River Phoenix

who played young indie in *Indiana Jones and the Last Crusade* died of a cocaine and morphine overdose in Johnny Depp's nightclub in October of 1993. His younger sister summer, who was only 14 at the time, and kind, were there, and contacted the authorities.

River and his younger brother and sisters were a part of a cult called

the children of God

a pseudo Christian cult with ties to NAMBLA that participates in

sexual and ritual abuse of children pedophilia and spouse swapping.

When the Phoenix family were found to have ties with a cult, the

mother immediately pulled her children from the cult and claimed

she believed it was just an innocent Christian group.

The cult is still active today under the name of the family international

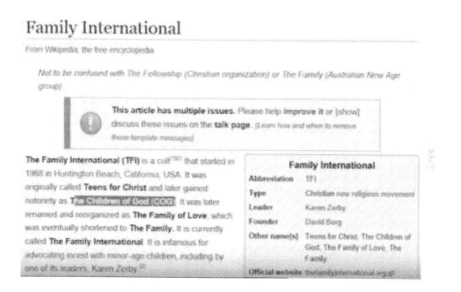

Family International

From Wikipedia, the free encyclopedia

Not to be confused with The Fellowship (Christian organization) or The Family (Australian New Age group).

> This article has multiple issues. Please help improve it or [show] discuss these issues on the talk page. *(Learn how and when to remove these template messages)*

The Family International (TFI) is a cult[citation] that started in 1968 in Huntington Beach, California, USA. It was originally called Teens for Christ and later gained notoriety as The Children of God (COG). It was later renamed and reorganized as The Family of Love, which was eventually shortened to The Family. It is currently called The Family International. It is infamous for advocating incest with minor-age children, including by one of its leaders, Karen Zerby.[citation]

Family International	
Abbreviation	TFI
Type	Christian new religious movement
Leader	Karen Zerby
Founder	David Berg
Other name(s)	Teens for Christ, The Children of God, The Family of Love, The Family
Official website	thefamilyinternational.org

They encourage children to masturbate while thinking about Jesus.

And finally Heather O'Rourke.

She was discovered in public by Steven Spielberg at the age of five

and cast in a horror film. *The Poltergeist.* She died in 1988, the

same year as Judith Barsi, at the age of 12 after she was

misdiagnosed with the flu.

But it was later reported that she died during surgery, to repair an acute bowel obstruction complicated by septic shock. This report was corroborated by the San Diego County coroner's office on February two days after her death.

Later reports changed the specific cause of death to cardiac arrest caused by septic shock brought on by the intestinal stenosis. This takes us to the final creepy fact about Steven Spielberg.

Number 1: Hollywood whispers

Heather's death at the time did not raise any alarms because it was misreported twice and with so many contradictions in the case of her death people started to question the original report. Many people now believe that Heather O'Rourke was abused and the autopsy report could be proof that she was abused. Intestinal stenosis or bowel obstruction is often caused by child abuse here is just one of many reports in the US National Library of Medicine to prove it.

Gastroenterol Clin. N Am. 2000 Nov 29; 19;[1-3] xl 5 abc 18;10(9)A baixado 2000-08-817 Epub 2000 Nov 19

Partial bowel obstruction in a 2-month-old child. A delayed diagnosis of anal abuse.

Apibo A[1], Casca E, Cecchetto G, Visli S, Magnato G, Gentile P.

⊕ Author information

Abstract

We present the case of an anal sexual abuse involving a 2-month-old boy who was admitted to the Pediatric Surgery Unit of the University of Padua for low bowel obstruction. The infant had been already hospitalized for 3 days in a peripheral hospital and treated with daily rectal wash-outs for a bezoarus. Only after a careful interpretation of the plain abdominal radiograph, along with the performance of a rectoscopy and a laparotomy, a vegetable foreign body (about 3 cm in diameter and 7 cm in length) was discovered in the sigma. The morphology and dimension of the foreign body, as well as its location, left no doubt about the etiology of the partial bowel obstruction, proving that it was clearly related to an anal sexual abuse!

PMID: 19757181   DOI: 10.1016/j.bpobgyn.2003.08.017

Indexed for MEDLINE]

Heather O'Rourke might have died from having a large object inserted into her anus and this is where things get weird.

Mind you the following article is unconfirmed and does not mention any name, however this user and lawyer was the same person who posted information about Harvey Weinstein and Kevin Spacey way before it broke the news. The blind titled *A Long Time Coming* reads, "When I started putting out feelers to former child actors who had worked on his movies I was surprised how many people wanted to tell their stories about working for this permanent A plus list director. They come from all different backgrounds and sexes. Most have never worked as adults as actors but a couple continue to make an effort and a couple have succeeded.

I started reaching out to them through an old friend a friend who once had a large role in a hit movie for the director, a friend who until recently never told me about the dark side to filming a movie with this legend. One thing he said resonated with me and I asked each of the others the same question. Most responded in the affirmative some said they wish they could remember but it had been X number of years or others said they really didn't want to think about it too much because it triggered them.

The query was whether the backstory of the character they were playing had molested. Their answer was yes. One actress who responded yes said she was only in the first grade when she made the movie. It had a lot of young kids in the movie although they were older than her. She remembers a cast "bonding" experience. All of the young actors and actresses were loaded onto a tour bus. Everyone was impressed because each seat on the bus had a DVD player waiting for them as a gift to take home.

Back then those things were expensive. The trip took about two hours from LA there were served all kinds of kids food on the bus. She remembers the all you could eat candy. So they get off the bus and arrive at this huge ranch. Who was there to greet them with the director? This permanent A plus list singer there were also other men there who she remembers hearing were studio executives. She doesn't know if they were she does remember walking around this carnival, as she put it, and seeing the executives pairing off with a couple of the actors or one on one. She says they later told her that most were molested or groped.

For her part she says she was just repeatedly groped. There was a carousel ride and one man insisted on putting her on a different horse each time. And he would lift her and grope her each time. She says she freaks out whenever she hears carousel music.

My friend from so long ago says his experience differed slightly. Another actress who was a teenager when she made a huge movie for the director, says that she wasn't given a ride on a tour bus, but instead was given a ride on a helicopter with her younger actor co-star. They ended up flying to that same ranch north of Los Angeles. When the helicopter landed that permanent A plus Lister was waiting there with the director. Also there was another actor from the movie who is probably B list today. The child actor was sent off with a group of men to the carnival while she was followed by the much older B-list actor who asked sexual questions one after the other and excused himself multiple times.

She assumes now that he was going off somewhere to pleasure himself and then come back after. It was hot that day and she remembers him drenched in sweat and just a pig in so many ways. She said she has talked to actors who didn't even get to act in the movie directed by the director but was still hired to help develop the backstory of the adult actors because they might use some flashback shots. All these actors added to the totals molested by the director and his friends.

Every movie seemed to have any kind of reason they could use to find teen boys and girls that could be molested under the guise of developing their character. Was the a-list director Steven Spielberg?

Was the LA Ranch Neverland?

Was the a-list singer Michael Jackson?

Was the movie *Hook?*

Was the little girl Amber Scott?

The youngest of the cast? Amber Scott never returned to acting

after *Hook.*

Michael Jackson was set to play Peter Pan in Spielberg's *Hook*.

Michael Jackson & Steven Spielberg

What happened? Steven Spielberg and Michael Jackson were very

close friends during the production of *Hook*. The connections are

there and they are strong. But wait it gets even darker. Yet another

blind appeared on the same site titled *Molesters killed her". Back

in the mid 80s was peak child-molesting time in Hollywood. There

was no internet. There were very very few mobile phones.

Children came to the set where they were left alone by their parents. For the next eight hours they were subject to every kind of horrible thing you can imagine. Drugs were commonplace. They were used to try and get the kids not to be so hysterical when being assaulted. Producers loved casting shows with kids and tweens. If someone pitched a show that involved a handful of tweens with a dozen tween extras per week, it would get a green light. Even if the show was going to suck, and everyone knew it was going to suck, if they got the right pedo at the studio, he would say yes just to come for the casting and taping of the pilot. As sad as it is to say, there were a lot of parents who told their kids to go off with a nice man in the suit and do what he says. It was a sick sick time. It was just past the mid-80s when a producer came up with the idea of a tween show that not only would feature our rotating cast of extras, but would make the studio a bunch of money because they would film quickly, and not hire any adults.

Further the faster they filmed the more time they would have to molest all the kids that would be hanging around. From the first day it was the worst place on earth if you were a kid. The studio where the show was filmed also had several other shows being filmed there. Most of which featured lots of children. Executives would drive over to Hollywood right before lunch and would stay at the studio for several hours each day. Anyway on this particular show there was a very special guest star still not a tween but everyone knew who she was. Executives flocked to the studio that day to see her. She was first molested when she was five or six and had continued to be molested throughout her hit movies and also on previous shows. One of the stars of the show who spent her life bouncing in and out of rehab because of what she saw, and who was actually nominated for awards from the show, described the atmosphere that day: "A bunch of fucking pigs.

I had just turned 12 or 13 I was the same age as the actress coming in. Maybe a little older. We had been shooting for months and I was old news. They knew I would do what they wanted but they always wanted someone new. This was someone new and someone they all knew. They had it set up like a Peep Show almost.

She had finished shooting that morning and they brought her out on a stage. The stage was used most of the time for a game show. That was taped there that game show is still on today. I can't watch it knowing what happened to her there. They brought her out and the front four rows of this theatre were filled with guys who were already rubbing themselves. This girl was wearing a bikini. The show took place around a beach just so they could make these girls wear next to nothing. They had her walk around under the lights the lights were focused on her and she couldn't really see out to the audience.

She was squinting it must have been blinding for her they had her walk back and forth. Then they had her start dancing all of these guys were doing what another star at the same studio got busted for. This went on for about 20 minutes. Then three of the guys took her to a different area of the studio. The actress didn't see what happened but 45 minutes later one of those three guys came running out and needed a set medic. Apparently they had inserted something inside the girl and things were bad. The medic came and the ambulance came. The parents of the girl were told some crappy story. That crap story ended up killing the girl because the parents believed the executives.

Two weeks later the show finished shooting six episodes all at once then everyone was sent on their way forever. No one wanted the kids around or any witnesses to what happened.

Was the young victim Heather O'Rourke?

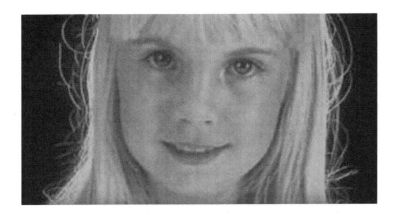

Was the show she was guest starring on *Rocky Road*?

Was it at Hollywood studios sunset Las Palmas?

Is the girl who witnessed this Devon Odessa?

Heather O'Rourke was discovered at the age of five by Steven

Spielberg.

She has been in several hit movies and became a bit of an icon as

the girl in front of the TV on *The Poltergeist.*

Her autopsy report states she suffered from bowel obstruction.

She was an extra on the show *Rocky Road*.

A show about some kids who inherit an ice-cream shop at the beach.

In 1987, when she was 11, she appeared in episode 22 season 3, which was filmed around April that same year. This show is filmed in Hollywood studio Sunset Las Palmas.

Jeopardy and *Rocky Road* were both shot at the same studio.

Devon Odessa starred in *Rocky Road*.

She was nominated as best young actress for her role in that show.

She has been in and out of rehab multiple times. The third season

of *Rocky Road* was the final season. There were 30 episodes in

season 3, which means they had to film the remaining eight to

finish the contract. As per The Blind it all seems to add up.

Is Steven Spielberg a member of NAMBLA? Does he like little boys? Is he a part of a child trafficking ring? And are his nefarious activities being covered up? Maybe, maybe no? After making these connection, although he certainly looks sinister, there is no proof that he is the big bad guy in Hollywood. And we will never know, unless someone speaks out about it. But even though he may not be directly involved, I do think it is safe to assume that he has some knowledge of what is really going on in Hollywood. If there are child trafficking or sex rings in Hollywood I am pretty certain he would know about them. Until more news breaks, it is very important that we keep asking questions and investigating. Because eventually the truth will come out!

And finally, if you found this book interesting and helpful, and you want more, I would be very grateful if you would consider leaving a review for the book on Amazon.

Just go to your account on Amazon. A free ebook version is also waiting for you as a paperback holder of this book!

Thank you and best further reading!

Made in the
USA
Middletown, DE